Sand Cats

Curious Kids Press

Sand Cats

There are only one species of the Sand Cat. This feline is also known as the Sand Dune Cat. This little animal was first discovered in 1858. Since then its numbers have dwindled. This cat looks a lot like our pet cats. However, it does have some very different traits. In this book we are going to explore many things about the Sand Cat. We will discover where this creature lives, its extraordinary abilities and so much more. Read on to be totally amazed with this cool cat.

Where in the World?

Did you know the sand cat is a true desert-dweller? It is found throughout the deserts of northern Africa and southwest and central Asia. It has to be specially adapted to live in this habitat. It lives in both sandy ground and stony desert. It can even be far from a water source.

The Body of a Sand Cat

Did you know the sand cat has a large head? However, its body is not all that large. It only measures from 15 to 20 inches long (39 to 52 centimeters). Its tail is quite long. It measures from 9.1 to 12.2 inches long (23.2 to 31 centimeters). This feline can weigh from 3 to 7.1 pounds (1.35 to 3.2 kilograms).

The Paws of a Sand Cat

Did you know this cat has special paws? Its paws need to be protected from the hot desert sand. The underside of the sand cat's paws are covered with thick fur - this keeps them from being burned. This cat also does not leave any footprints in the sand.

The Eyes and Ears of a Sand Cat

Did you know this cat has large eyes? They are a greenish-yellow color and are surrounded by a white ring. Its pointed ears are positioned on the side of its head. This gives the sand cat an excellent sense of hearing. This helps it hunt for food and to stay safe from predators.

Sand Cat's Fur

Did you know sand cats in the northern regions have long fur in the wintertime? This fur can grow up to 2 inches in length (5.1 centimeters). The sand cat needs long fur to help keep it warm. The color of the cat's coat is a pale sandy color. The lower and upper lips, chin, throat and belly are white. It also have black markings on it.

What a Sand Cat Eats

Did you know sand cat is a carnivore? This means it eats meat. The sand cat will hunt and dine on small rodents like mice, gerbils and jerboas. It will also hunt birds like the desert lark. This feline has also been observed hunting reptiles, sand vipers and nsects.

How the Sand Cat Hunts

Did you know the sand cat uses all its senses to locate its prey? It uses its big ears and excellent hearing to hear its prey, even if its underground. In fact, the sand cat can dig very quickly to extract its prey from the ground. This cat will also bury any leftovers to eat later.

Sand Cat Burrows

Did you know the sand cat will use the burrow of other animals? It will use the abandoned burrows of the fox or the porcupine. It will also enlarge the burrows of gerbils or other rodents. It uses the burrows to escape the heat of the sun.

Sand Cat Talk

Did you know the sand cat can make sounds similar to a pet cat? It can meow, growl, hiss and purr. Along with these sounds, it can also make a short rasping bark. It does this when looking for a mate or trying to locate other sand cats.

The Sand Cat's Special Ability

Did you know this cat can run very fast? It can run from 19 to 25 miles-per-hour (30 to 40 kilometers-per-hour) but only for a short distance. It also has a special way of moving. It will walk with its belly to the ground. It will also move quickly with the occasional leap added in.

Sand Cat Mom

Did you know the female sand cat is pregnant from 59 to 63 days? She can have from 2 to 4 kittens. Mom sand cat feeds her kittens milk from her body. At 5 weeks-old, she will begin to feed them meat from her hunts. She protects her young until they are ready to be on their own.

Sand Cat Babies

Did you know newborn sand cats have spotted pale yellow or reddish fur? The kittens are totally dependent on mom sand cat for food and protection. The kittens are only ready to be one their own after 6 to 8 months. Sand cat kittens are ready to have their own families at around 12 months-of-age.

Predators of the Sand Cat

Did you know this animal has many natural predators? The sand cat's main predators are wild dogs, snakes, birds of prey and humans. The loss of habitat is also putting this small feline at risk. Farmers moving in on their territory cuts down on the cat's ability to hunt rodents.

Life of a Sand Cat

Did you know the sand cat prefers to be left alone? It is a solitary animal that only gets together during the breeding season. Males always live alone, while the mother sand cat will look after her young. After her young are old enough to leave, she will live alone until the next batch of kittens.

Sand Cats in Zoos

Did you know sand cats can survive up to 13 years in captivity? However, they rarely live that long. Sand cats in zoos do not do very well. Only 41 percent of captive bred sand cat kittens makes it to adulthood. Zoos are doing their best to change this and are trying to learn more about this desert feline.

Quiz

Question 1: Where is the sand cat Found?

Answer 1: In the desert

Question 2: What is special about the sand Cat's feet?

Answer 2: The bottoms are covered in thick fur and they do not leave any footprints

Question 3: The sand cat is a carnivore. What does that mean?

Answer 3: It eats meat

Question 4: What type of abandoned home will the sand cat take over?

Answer 4: Burrows

Question 5: How many kittens does the female sand cat give birth to?

Answer 5: 2 to 4

Thank you for checking out another title from Curious Kids Press! Make sure to search "Curious Kids Press" on Amazon.com for many other great books.

Made in the USA
Middletown, DE
02 May 2022